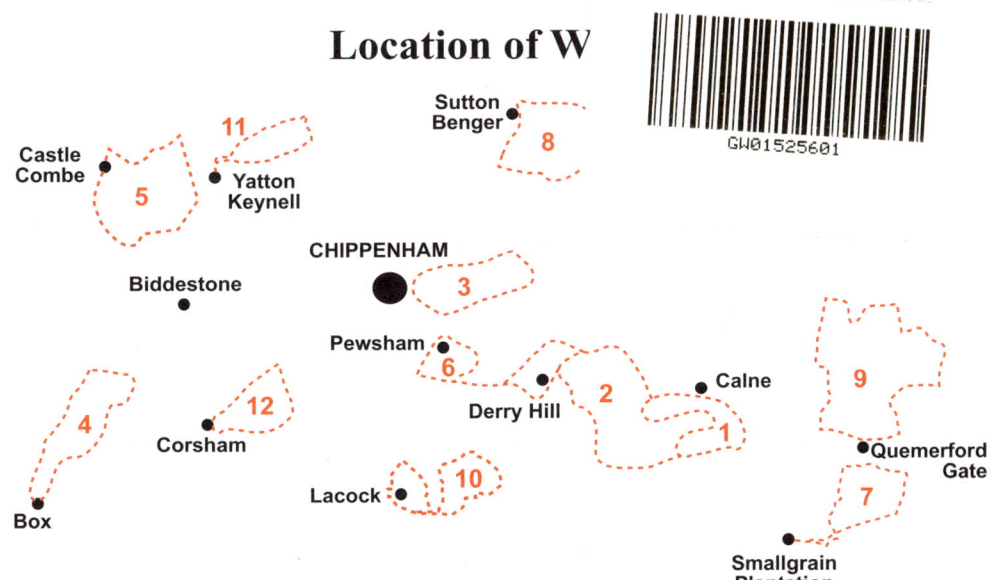

Ordnance Survey Maps

It is advisable to use Ordnance Survey Maps in conjunction with the sketch maps in this book, but occasionally there will be a discrepancy between the two because of changes that have occurred on the ground and are not yet shown on the OS Maps. The sketch maps attempt to show a route that is correct at the time of publication.

Ordnance Survey maps can be bought at local bookshops or borrowed from public libraries.

The OS maps required for the walks described in this book are:

Explorer No. 156	Chippenham and Bradford-on-Avon (1:25,000)
Explorer No. 157	Marlborough and Savernake Forest (1:25,000)
Landranger No. 173	Swindon and Devizes (1:50,000)

Problems on Paths

If you find any problems such as damaged stiles, fallen trees or obstructed paths, please report the exact location to:

MyWiltshire App

or Wiltshire Council, Rights of Way and Countryside, County Hall, Trowbridge,
   Wiltshire, BA14 8JN or email rightsofway@wiltshire.gov.uk

or phone the local RoW warden on 01249 468567 or 07771 721255

or use the Wiltshire.gov.uk website to "Report a highways problem"

and/or Ramblers Central Office online via www.ramblers.org.uk/pathproblem

WALKS INDEX

Walk		Distance	Page
1	**Calne and Black Dog Bridge**	5½ miles	6
	looks at the quieter side of Calne to the south and west.		
2	**Derry Hill, Calne and Bowood**	8 miles	8
	starts from Derry Hill and visits Calne and the Bowood estate.		
3	**The Anscombe Trail**	4½ miles	10
	explores some of the paths between Chippenham and Tytherton Lucas.		
4	**Weavern, By Brook, Box and Rudloe**	6½ miles	12
	a pretty meadow and woodland walk to the north east of Box.		
5	**Castle Combe and By Brook**	5½ miles	14
	reveals some of the delightful countryside around Castle Combe.		
6	**Pewsham, Derry Hill and Bowood**	7 miles	16
	uses paths to the east of Chippenham and allows a visit to the Lansdowne Arms at Derry Hill for refreshments.		
7	**Cherhill and The Wansdyke**	7 miles	18
	a mainly downland walk to the south east of Calne and includes the Cherhill Monument and White Horse.		
8	**Sutton Benger and Christian Malford**	4 miles	20
	takes in Sutton Benger and Christian Malford; orchids in an SSSI may be seen in springtime.		
9	**Quemerford, Compton Bassett and Cherhill**	8 miles	22
	goes east of Calne and to the higher plateau above Compton Bassett where distant views may be had to the east.		
10	**Lacock, Bowden Hill and Naish Hill**	4/5 miles	24
	a figure-of-eight walk from the well known National Trust village of Lacock and climbs up to Bowden Hill with views over the Avon valley.		
11	**Yatton Keynell and Easton Piercy**	4 miles	26
	starts from the Bell Inn, Yatton Keynell and visits Easton Piercy.		
12	**Corsham, Easton and Corsham Park**	3½ miles	28
	starts from Corsham and takes in Corsham Park.		

12 Walks around Chippenham

These walks were devised to take you to the best vantage points in the area and to bring you back to your starting point. The routes are easy to follow using visible paths or other features described in the text or on the maps and, with noted exceptions, follow public rights of way. Where they do not, permission has been obtained to use the path or it is known to have been in use for at least 20 years.

Wet weather can make paths muddy and the summer months can bring brambles and nettles, so it is important to be suitably dressed and to wear sensible footwear. A light pair of secateurs can be handy for removing brambles, particularly around stiles. During autumn, paths across fields can become obscured by ploughing before the farmer reinstates them.

Most of the walks cross roads and some use roads to link up footpaths. When walking on roads it is usually safer to walk on the right hand side in single file.

Production by Rob Dawson

Cover picture ©2010 by Gill Minter

Originally published by the Chippenham Group of the Ramblers in 2004

Revised and reprinted in 2010
to commemorate the 75th Anniversary of the Ramblers (1935-2010)
and in memory of departed members of the Chippenham Group.
Reprinted 2013

Revised and Reprinted in 2018
by the North West Wiltshire Group of the Ramblers

Printed in England by Corsham Print
Unit 4, Leafield Way, Leafield Industrial Estate, Corsham, Wiltshire, SN13 9SW
Tel. 01225 812 930, Fax 01225 819 221
email: info@corshamprint.co.uk
Website: www.corshamprint.co.uk

Printed on paper produced from sustainable forests

This publication, or parts thereof, may not be reproduced, stored in a retrieval system, or transmitted in any form or by any method or purpose, electronic, mechanical, photocopying, recording or otherwise without the prior specific authority in writing of the North West Wiltshire Group of the Ramblers.

Disclaimer

Every effort has been made to ensure the accuracy of the information in this booklet but the Ramblers cannot accept any responsibilty for any changes which affect the routes described or for the consequences.

Walk 1   Calne and Black Dog Bridge
contributed by Kath Parkinson and Roger Barnes

Starting Point: Calne Sports Centre car park. It is possible to start at the Town Hall where most buses stop (point **[A]** in the text).
Grid Reference: ST 998700
OS Maps: Explorer 156 and 157; Landranger 173
Distance: 5½ miles or 9 kilometres
Time required: 2½ to 3 hours
Parking: Free at the Sports Centre, please park furthest away from the Centre.
Bus: Regular service 55 between Chippenham Rail/Bus Stations and Calne. Alight at Calne Town Hall and start walk at point **[A]** in the text.
Refreshments: Available in Calne.
Introduction: This walk shows the quieter side of the Town along with the open country. It includes part of the old railway line from Calne to Chippenham, now a cycle track.
One place can be very wet and muddy even during good weather.

Walk Description:

From car park head off down closed-off road past LH side of sports centre. On reaching A4, cross to path on opposite side of road. Turn R and go through avenue of trees past church to path off to L (between church and school).

Follow this narrow path with care as it gets steeper. At end walk over to bridge across River Marden **(DO NOT CROSS) (1)**. Turn L and follow river, there is a path between river and back fence of some gardens. Continue along this path until reaching tarmac road (Brewers Lane). Go up hill to just before road junction; where, on opposite side of road, is another path. Go down steps and once again follow river keeping L at any forks in path until arriving out on road again. Turn L. The town centre is entered now. Follow road up hill to The Green **(2)**. Off to R is St Mary's church. Head towards church passing numerous listed buildings. Follow road around to L of church and then R to soon come to traffic lights by Town Hall **[A]**.

Cross road and climb Cox's Hill between Town Hall and Lansdowne Hotel. Follow this road past Baptist church on L. The road continues straight, narrowing before coming to kissing gate; go through and follow straight narrow path to hedge; there are kissing gates on L and on R. Follow path to R keeping hedge on L, go across private drive, follow path, then across stile on R into open field **(3)**.

Look up hill to where a gate and a stile can be seen; head diagonally across field towards stile, past a water trough on R.

Go over stile and one on opposite side of track. Head off in the direction of twelve o'clock, which will just miss trees on R, as next stile is well out of sight and approximately half way down the hill **(4)**.

Go over this stile on to A4 **(take great care!)**. Follow road downhill to a track to L just before bridge across A4.

Go up this track and through gates at top *(the smoke is the gate opener)* **(5)** to join the Calne to Chippenham cycle track, which follows the old Calne branch railway line. Turn L

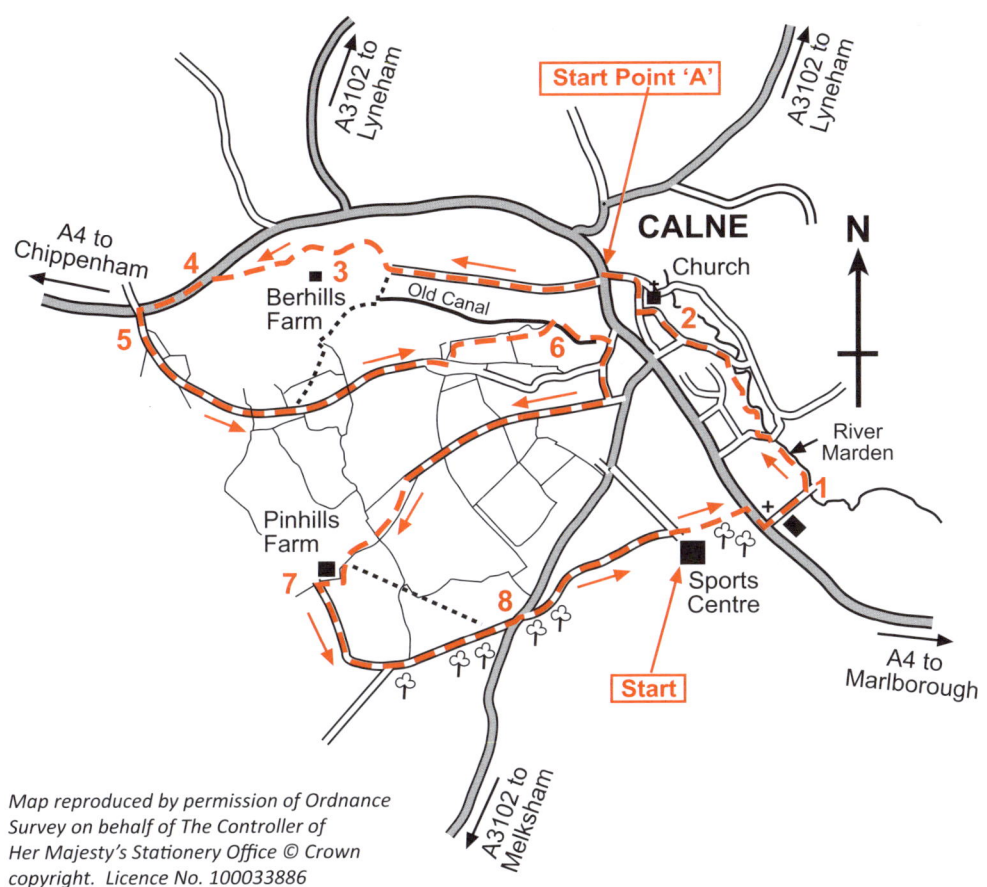

and go along track for 1 mile before track starts to descend.

Continue on along track and through steel kissing gate. After crossing brick-built bridge **(6)** turn R and follow canal until coming to road.

Turn R. At Fire Station carefully cross road and take path opposite. At top of path turn R and follow this track to blue and white footpath sign just before two houses at end of track.

Follow sign on L past back of houses and go straight up track and up L side of field to bridge and stile. Follow footpath sign to go uphill, over stile on L and then R along edge of field to a tarmac track **(7)**.

Turn L and follow tarmac track away from farm through some trees; keep L on meeting another track. At end of track is main road, go straight across and through remains of a gateway **(8)**. Follow track *(which can be muddy!)* down to car park.

If the walk was started at the Town Hall carry on to point **(A)** as detailed in the first part of this text.

Walk 2   Derry Hill, Calne and Bowood

contributed by Adrian Stovell and Alan Roberts

Starting Point: Large lay-by on the A4, 4 miles from Chippenham towards Calne, on left 300 yards before the Studley/Derry Hill crossroads.
Grid Reference: ST 959711
OS Maps: Explorer 156; Landranger 173
Distance: 8 miles or 13 kilometres
Time required: 3 to 3½ hours
Parking: At the starting point lay-by.
Bus: Regular service 55 between Chippenham Rail/Bus Stations and Calne. Alight at Studley / Derry Hill cross roads and walk back down the hill to the lay-by.
Refreshments: Available in Calne or at Lansdowne Arms, Derry Hill
Introduction: The walk includes a section of the old Calne branch railway line, now a cycle track. The route goes through the beautiful Bowood estate.

Walk Description:

From lay-by walk up A4, up hill to large field gate on L under some trees **(1)**. Go through gate and, keeping fence on R, follow edge of field to bottom corner. Skirt house ahead and bear round to R to join lane. Turn R on lane and take L fork after a few yards.

At T-junction bear L into Norley Lane and continue to fork **(2)**. Bear L signposted Hazeland. *(Notice the Lansdowne Monument and Cherhill White Horse on hills to R.)* After small bridge, go through gate on R and follow cycleway formed from the former Chippenham to Calne railway line. *(Watch for cyclists!.)*

Continue to cantilevered bridge over A4 **(3)**. *(At other side there are some old railway buildings and platforms that were once Black Dog Halt.)*

Follow cycle way for some while, and after track turns to tarmac surface go down slope, through gateway and along bottom of field to gate/cattle grid. Go through gate and across brick-built bridge over Wilts and Berks Canal **(4)**.

After crossing bridge turn R and follow path below stone wall. *(The mound on L is site of Calne Castle.)* Go along this path, following canal, and bear R at old canal boat to cross River Marden, and emerge onto Station Road.

Turn R and follow road to Fire Station **(5)**. Opposite Fire Station is a narrow tarmac path, follow this to top of hill. At top turn R and follow lane out into countryside where it becomes a rough tarmac track.

On leaving built-up area there are a couple more houses on hill ahead. Just before these follow small blue footpath signs to L past houses, then bear R onto upper field to far hedge.

Cross plank bridge and stile, keep to L of field as signposted and uphill, turning L at another sign by an oak tree before Pinhills Farm.

Cross stile and turn R to follow top of field and hedge, skirting farm and heading towards bungalow. At tarmac farm road, follow it L away from farm.

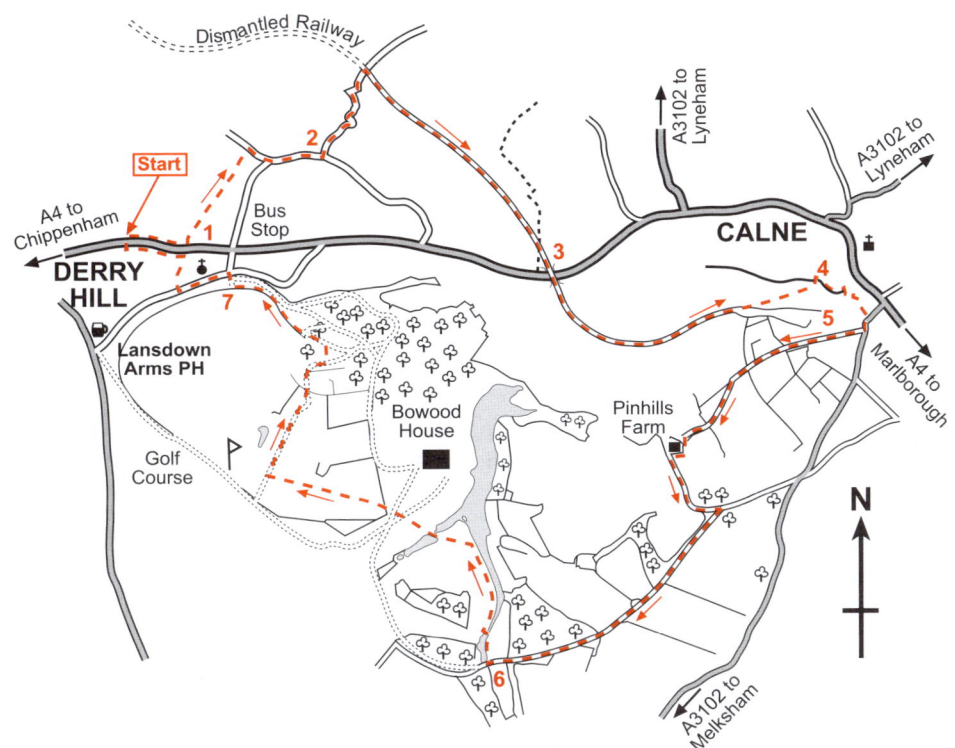

Map reproduced by permission of Ordnance Survey on behalf of The Controller of Her Majesty's Stationery Office © Crown copyright. Licence No. 100033886

At road junction turn R and follow for 1 mile. Just before balustraded stone bridge **(6)** go through metal kissing gate on R and follow lake overflow for 200 yards to stone bridge.

Cross bridge and follow lake edge northwards for 500 yards. *(Bowood House is visible ahead.)*

Follow bank as it bends L and go through metal kissing gate at blue marker. Once across lake continue up to brow of hill.

Turn L briefly on track until it bends, then go up to kissing gate in wire fence ahead. Go through gate and turn R for 50 yards, then L as signed across field in direction of poplar copse. Pass this and keep to L of fence to kissing gate.

Go through and turn R on tarmac path alongside golf course for 400 yards. When path bends R at a mirror, keep straight on and follow signs through wood, bearing L at barns to go downhill under telephone wires. Cross plank bridge and turn L. Go uphill beside golf course; at top of slope bear R through trees, continuing to R of old iron fence for 400 yards to a gap in trees. Turn R through gap to estate gates **(7)**. Leave Bowood through gate, turn L along Church Road passing a school on R; immediately after school take footpath on R. *(If wishing to visit the Lansdowne Arms, continue along Church Road to pass Golden Gate on L and pub is opposite.)*

At new Village Hall continue straight on to meet the A4. Turn L and follow A4 down hill to car or up hill to bus stop.

Walk 3   The Anscombe Trail

contributed by Gill Minter and Roger Barnes

Starting Point: Olympiad Leisure Centre car park *(pay and display)*, Sadlers Mead, Chippenham. *(This is near the railway station.)*
Grid Reference: ST 923736
OS Maps: Explorer 156; Landranger 173
Distance: 4½ miles or 7 kilometres
Time required: 2½ hours
Parking: As above or various town centre car parks. No facilities on this walk.
Refreshments: Café and toilets are available in the Wiltshire Council offices next to Olympiad Leisure Centre.
Introduction: A circular walk to Tytherton Lucas using mainly field paths and tracks to north east of Chippenham, crossing the Rivers Avon and Marden. When river is high, use alternative route from **(8)**.

Walk Description:

Leave car park via pedestrian path in back LH corner leading into Monkton Park **(1)**.

After 30 yards fork R and follow surfaced path downhill and L alongside river to Crazy Golf course. Pass bridge and continue on to 2nd bridge **(2)** *(painted blue)*; cross bridge and immediately turn L into field by display board. Take path to R corner into playing field. Cross to far hedgerow next to children's play area.

Go through gap in hedge beyond playground and onto rough track. Straight ahead and climb stile to the R of the white painted Sea Cadets H.Q. **(3)**.

Head across this field to stile in far L corner, under power lines, then keeping hedge on L, follow path to next stile-gate. Continue across next field to R of farmhouse and over stile onto lane.

Turn L and follow lane past farm barns and uphill 700 yards to cross the cycleway **(4)**. Carry on straight ahead for 200 yards across field to stile *(to R of bungalow)* in opposite hedge. Cross next field, aiming for middle telegraph pole, then straight on down slope, through gap and over stile, then on another 100 yards to "Anscombe's" bridge over the Marden **(5)**.

Cross bridge and bear R along river bank 100 yards before bearing L alongside hedge away from river. At far side of field go through gap and with hedge now on L, cross this field to road at Tytherton Lucas **(6)**. Turn L on grass verge, walk past gate to St. Nicholas's Church and take farm track past staddlestones in front of Manor Farm stables keeping to R of stream. The River Avon is reached after 500 yards **(7)**.

Cross river footbridge on R and continue straight ahead 300 yards to far hedge, through small metal gate and over stone bridge over pools. Go a few more yards along this track before taking path on L over plank bridge into field **(8)****. With trees on L, carry on straight ahead for about 250 yards before riverside path veers R alongside river over stile and through gap in hedge towards copse. Follow path through copse and downhill to river.

At stile, path veers 45° R away from river, to stile and wooden bridge near top end of mature hedgerow **(9)**. Cross bridge and keep hedgerow on your R for 500 yards to next footbridge/stile in top far corner of field. Go over these. Follow path diagonally R 200 yards past pylon on L to stile, carry on again veering R 200 yards to stile at hedge leading out onto Cocklebury Lane **(10)**.

Follow lane L, over cycleway to Calne to reach Eastern Avenue. Follow this then turn R on Cocklebury Road, continue past Wiltshire College to Sadlers Mead and turn L to Olympiad start point.

Alternative route when river is high. At **(8), avoid potentially flooded route through copse. Having crossed plank bridge strike off diagonally across two fields to barns, emerging on lane. Turn L past houses. Skirt L of pond and continue below Upper Peckingell farm into field. Go straight across field under telegraph pole to double stile and plank bridge one third up far hedge. Continue southwest towards tall thin pylon to reach stile and wooden bridge near top end of mature hedgerow at **(9)**. Continue on main walk route.

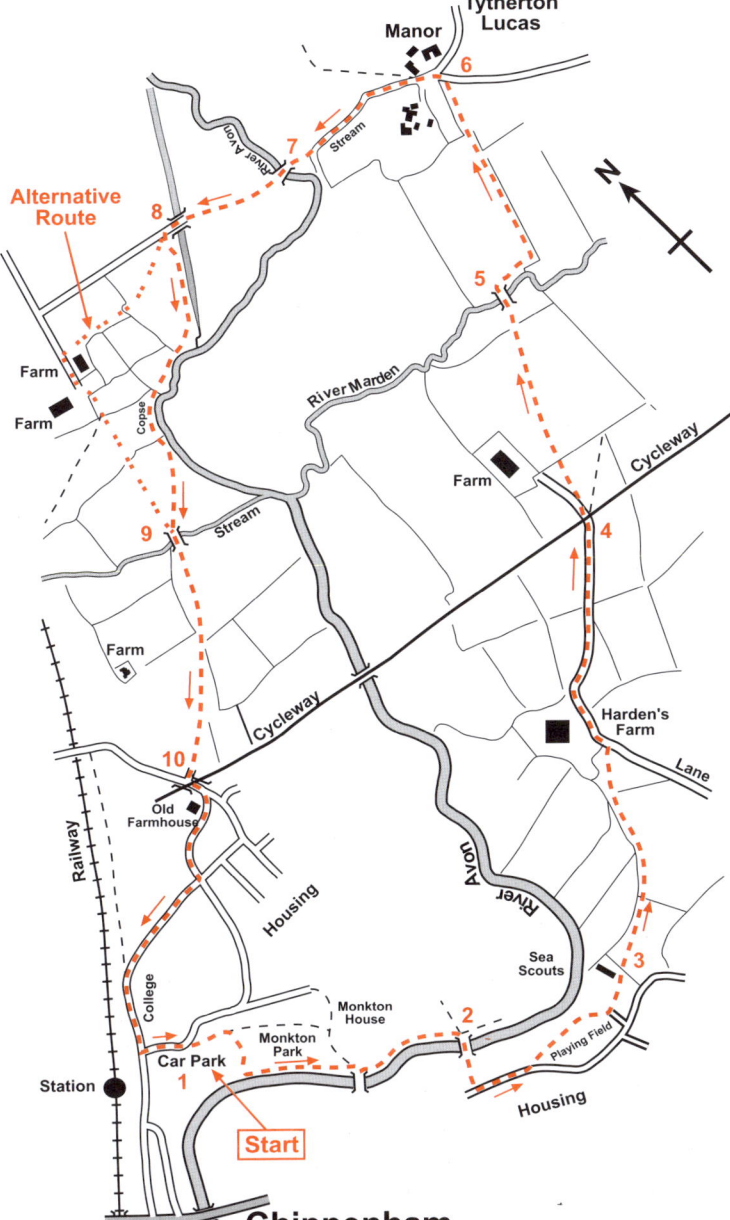

Map reproduced by permission of Ordnance Survey on behalf of The Controller of Her Majesty's Stationery Office © Crown copyright. Licence No. 100033886

Walk 4   Weavern, By Brook, Box and Rudloe

contributed by Gill Minter and Judy Hible

Starting Point:	Box Library / Selwyn Hall car park, Box
Grid Reference:	ST 824686
OS Maps:	Explorer 156; Landranger 173
Distance:	6½ miles or 10 kilometres
Time required:	3½ hours
Parking:	As above.
Bus:	Regular service X31 between Chippenham Bus/Rail Stations and Bath, stops at top of lane to Selwyn Hall.
Refreshments:	Pubs in Box, café by Post Office
Introduction:	A pretty meadow and woodland walk with a couple of moderate hills, following the By Brook and using part of the MacMillan Way.

Walk Description:

Start from LH corner of car park **(1)**, walk down steps to stream and turn R onto track. Continue to gate onto Mill Lane. Turn L and walk under railway bridge, immediately turn R up footpath **(2)**. Pass timber yard. On reaching drive turn R for a few yards then immediately L opposite garage wall through iron posts.

Bear L at seat, and just before meeting main road bear L again towards 16-11 The Bassetts. Follow signs along laurel hedge and across field. Turn L down drive past Acorn and Oakleaf cottages **(3)**, to top corner of lawn and cross stile.

Follow path at upper side of field. At river bend after an awkward stile, bear slightly R uphill to avoid swamp, then downhill again under telephone wires to stile at bottom of far hedge.

Continue beside brook, keeping on path, through yard and between houses to mill **(4)**. At lane, take wooden gate diagonally opposite. Follow direction of sign L of telephone pole, and turn R on meeting hedge to reach stile on L across brook.

Turn R with hedge on R, over stile under hazel tree. Bear L round bottom edge of slope to bottom of copse **(5)**. Follow gully leftwards below copse and over stile under big field maple with footpath sign on it pointing way diagonally uphill.

Head for cottages top L, cross stile and head uphill round edge of garden. On reaching lane **(6)**, turn L. At fork, turn L on No Through Road and continue on lane. *(After wooden garage note view through gap to Bath.)*

Keep on tarmac lane. Continue straight on when tarmac ends. Soon after passing pylon and entering wood, fork R AFTER wooden gate **(7)** and before path plunges downhill.

Go downhill and up again, bearing R to reach metalled lane **(8)**. Turn L downhill, at bottom take incised bridleway **(9)** on L before metal gate.

On reaching stream, go straight through gate. At footbridge **(10)** bear L uphill along lower edge of wood on the MacMillan Way. Pass through wooden gate and after 100 yards another gate and continue straight on following the line of the By Brook.

On reaching Widdenham Farm **(11)** follow lane away from farm for 200 yards to bend in road **(12)**. Take bridle path into field and follow stream bank to metal gate onto lane at farm.

Turn L on lane **(13)** for 50 yards then fork R. After 20 yards, cross stile on L after wooden gate **(14)**, and then another stile a short way on, at bottom corner of field.

Follow the MacMillan Way for ½ mile, past houses on opposite bank, to stile at river end of fence. Turn R as per sign, by waterfall, past Studios to road. Turn L **(15)** for 50 yards, then R at kissing gate **(16)** just after railway bridge. Follow stream to small bridge on L, cross and turn R onto track then retrace outward route back to car park.

Walk 5

Castle Combe and By Brook

contributed by David Crook and Alan Roberts

Starting Point: Castle Combe car park (in upper Castle Combe, just off B4039)
Grid Reference: ST 845777
OS Maps: Explorer 156; Landranger 173
Distance: 5½ miles or 9 kilometres
Time required: 2½ to 3 hours
Parking: As above.
Bus: Service 35/35A from Chippenham Bus/Rail Stations every 2 hours approx. (not Sundays or public holidays).
Refreshments: Pubs in Castle Combe (and public toilets).
Introduction: A pleasant walk on both quiet country lanes and footpaths, visiting the well-known village of Castle Combe and the hamlet of Long Dean with stretches of the By Brook. This walk can be muddy in or after wet weather. (Areas near the motor racing circuit may be noisy on race days.)

Walk Description:

Leaving car park turn L uphill to main road (B4039) **(1)**. Turn L onto grass verge and follow for 50 yards, cross road with care and turn R into lane.

Continue along this lane for 800 yards to byway crossing **(2)**. Take byway on R *(Summer Lane)* to meet B4039. Turn L into lane for 400 yards, towards water tower in distance, and round sharp bend. Just before next bend **(3)** go over stile on R by cottage.

Follow footpath, passing two lakes, to stile onto B4039 **(4)**; go diagonally R across road to small gate and join bridleway. Continue along this path for 800 yards *(passing Kent's Bottom Farm)* along bottom of valley, going through three gates on way. Bear slightly R and enter Hammerdown Wood via gate **(5)** at bridleway sign.

Proceed 400 yards through wood and exit by another gate, to bear R along RH slope of valley for another 400 yards before entering lane through gate. Go L and almost immediately fork R into the hamlet of Long Dean **(6)**.

Turn R at post box *(note that it is a rare Victorian one)* and join the Macmillan Way. At this point it is rough track that rises, then gradually descends for 1 mile before crossing flat stone bridge over the By Brook onto road in Castle Combe **(7)**.

Turn R to walk through village *(passing public toilets on L)* and fork L at the Market Cross **(8)**, passing The Castle Inn and under archway *(signed Public Footpath)*. Follow lane L, then R uphill on stony track to reach small gate **(9)**. Turn R *(the Macmillan Way turns L here)* onto uphill footpath.

At golf course follow stone wall on R, path shortly bears L away from wall to pass between bushes on L and wire fence on R. Follow path to end of fence to enter a tarmac lane, passing the old school on L to reach road. Turn L uphill, then forking first L **(10)** back to car park.

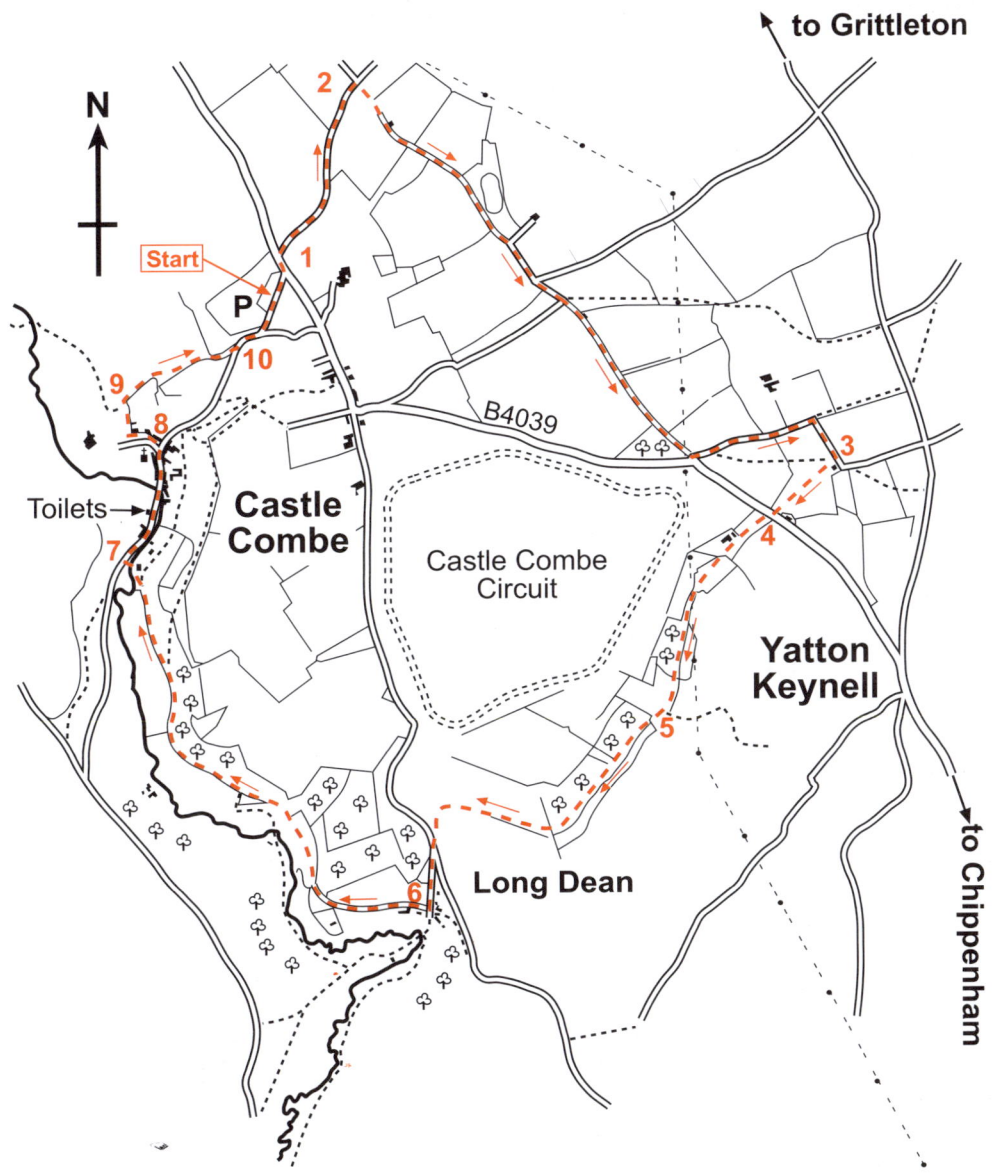

Walk 6   Pewsham, Derry Hill and Bowood

contributed by Gill Minter and Bob Maddick

Starting Point: Pewsham shopping centre, (junction of Lodge Road and Canal Road behind the Old Lane pub)
Grid Reference: ST 930720
OS Maps: Explorer 156; Landranger 173
Distance: 7 miles or 11 kilometres
Time required: 3½ to 4 hours
Parking: Car park for local shopping centre.
Bus: Regular service 44P from Chippenham Bus Station to Pewsham shops (not Sundays or public holidays).
Refreshments: Available at the Lansdowne Arms **(13)** and the Lysley Arms **(6)**.
Introduction: A circular walk with the central part climbing to Bowood Park with good long-distance views and crossing the Wilts and Berks Canal.

Walk Description:

Walk along service road to roundabout **(1)** and turn L on Blackthorn Mews for 100 yards. Take Forest Lane to R, past nursery and vets. Cross Pewsham Way and take lane opposite towards Lodge Farms **(2)**.

At cottages **(3)**, turn L on tarmac lane. Pass farm and keep straight on along green lane.

At the Wilts and Berks Canal cross lock and stile **(4)**, then follow L hedge line. Go through gap ahead and straight across field to cross tarmac track keeping close to hedge on R **(5)** to gate in field corner. Continue with hedge on R, then diagonally across field to stile on L at near end of copse. Cross the Lysley Arms car park to main road.

Cross A4 **(6)** and take roadside path uphill to edge of wood. Enter field on L just after national speed limit sign **(7)** and follow field edge below wood. At end of 2nd field path enters wood. Go R and then immediately L. A new path lies between wood and field fence, keep fence to your L. Continue past cottage to road **(8)**. *(In fields on opposite side of road is site of Stanley*

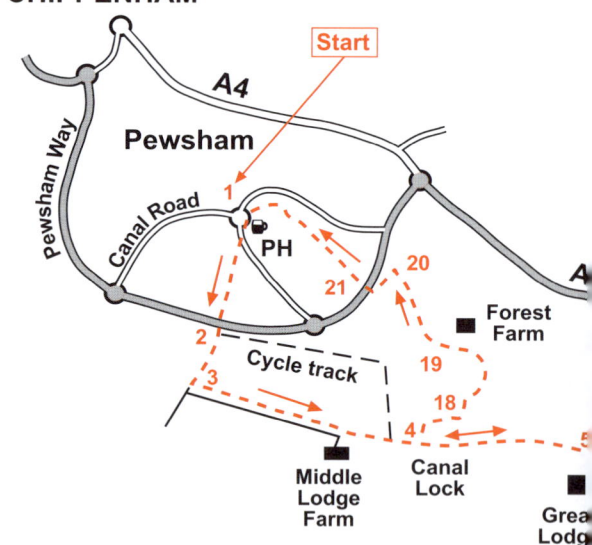

Map reproduced by permission of Ordnance Survey on behalf of The Control

Abbey, suppressed by Henry VIII in 1536.) At road, turn R up hill into Studley. Near top of hill, opposite bungalow "Badgers Holt" **(9)** turn R past footpath sign and "The Drock" into small group of houses. Bear L at No's 98/99, around garage and alongside garden, continuing straight on keeping timber yard on your L, to meet the A4 **(10)**.

Cross A4 and take path opposite, past housing, village hall and school on your L to meet Derry Hill Church Road **(11)**. Turn L past church and school, then at the bend turn R through gate into Bowood estate. *(Small gate is open if Bowood House is closed.)* At fence **(12)** turn R alongside golf course. At the end of golf course exit by Golden Gate on R **(13)**. Here you can stop for a break at the Lansdowne Arms pub or cross the main Devizes road and take waymarked path opposite between hedges **(14)**. Go over stile, across field, through gate and down wooden steps.

Continue down hill over far stile and into a conservation area. Carry on down towards stream, but don't be lured by bridge at bottom of valley; instead look for an open gate in RH hedge about half way down. Follow well-used path to field corner, across bridge **(15)**. Continue along bottom of hill to stile/bridge in far hedge some way below farm **(16)**. Turn R towards houses and head for electricity pylons, go R over stile between houses. Turn L down old road **(17)** to the Lysley Arms.

Retrace route through pub car park **(6)**, over stile in corner to cross field diagonally L and continue with hedge on L. Cross tarmac track **(5)** and straight across field to gap. Keep hedge on your R and follow hedge line back to canal lock **(4)**. Cross canal bridge. At this point **EITHER** join cycle path 403 ahead and follow it back to point **(2)** **OR** turn R alongside canal lock, going through small wood and over stile. Keeping hedge on L, follow hedge line around field corner to stile with concrete step before clump of trees **(18)**. Go over this stile and head for waymarked stile in opposite hedge, L of farm **(19)**. Bear L of hedge on brow of hill and continue keeping hedge on R through gate and over stile to emerge on grassy patch by Pewsham Way **(20)**. Turn L and continue to stile by a tree and then cross road to take tarmac path **(21)** between metal barrier's and back to service road.

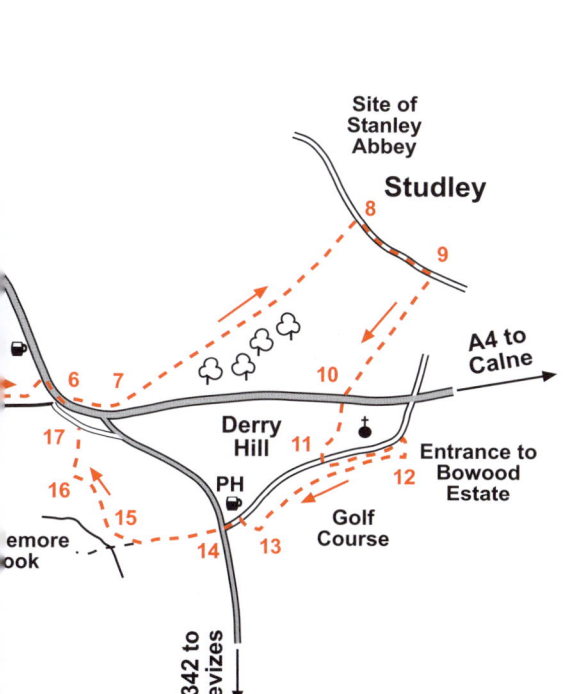

Majesty's Stationery Office © Crown copyright. Licence No. 100033886

Walk 7   Cherhill and The Wansdyke

contributed by Roger Barnes and Judy Hible

Starting Point:	The picnic site at 'Smallgrain Plantation' on the minor road between the A4 at Quemerford in Calne and the A361.
Grid Reference:	SU 019671
OS Maps:	Explorer 157; Landranger 173
Distance:	7 miles or 11 kilometres
Time required:	3½ to 4 hours
Parking:	Ample off-road parking at the picnic site as above.
Bus:	None
Refreshments:	None
Introduction:	A mainly downland walk taking in a small section of the Wansdyke, Morgan's Hill Nature Reserve, the Cherhill Monument, Oldbury Hill Fort and the Roman Road. This walk can be muddy in places and there are a couple of climbs, one quite steep.

Walk Description:

Leave picnic site from LH end, *(stand with back to road)* by walking up steps and grass bank at about 11 o'clock, towards trees to join the Wansdyke **(1)**. *(This, now mostly obliterated trenched embankment running from near Portishead to near Marlborough, was probably constructed in the 5th/6th centuries to keep out Saxon invaders from the north.)*

Turn R and follow the Wansdyke for 200 yards then go through gate on R leading into Morgan's Hill Nature Reserve. Follow this path *(Wansdyke)* uphill until two large radio masts come into sight. At top of hill, when you reach large gate, turn L onto path, which leads across to small gate. Go through this – *(you are still in the Nature Reserve and may see Orchids and Butterflies in summer)*. Follow path, keeping high up along contour of hill. *(You can see the Roman Road below L and good views across the valley.)* When you get to wooden gate straight ahead, turn down path on L in front of it and go through gate onto the Roman Road. Cross stile directly opposite **(2)**.

Go down side of hill keeping hedge on L, until you reach small copse at bottom. Turn L and follow track round and down, keeping copse on your R until you reach two gates on your R. Go through then shortly look for gate on L. Go through then bear R across field towards Calstone Wellington Church looking for stile in fence onto track beyond. Follow track past church on R down to road in Calstone **(3)**.

Turn R and walk along road then through entrance to South Farm. Take LH of two paths in 50 yards, bear L, cross stream, then immediately take RH fork uphill.

Follow path uphill until it reaches lane **(4)**. Turn R and follow this lane for about 25 yards uphill. When lane bears R keep straight on along path, which runs along edge of field with fence on L. Keep straight on through two gates – about ¾ mile – until path reaches barn on L **(5)**. Go through gate then turn R onto path in an enclosed lane (sometimes overgrown) and follow this uphill. After about ½ mile this enclosed green lane veers R and comes to gate and stile.

Go through. A sign here indicates Cherhill Down. Continue uphill on well-trodden

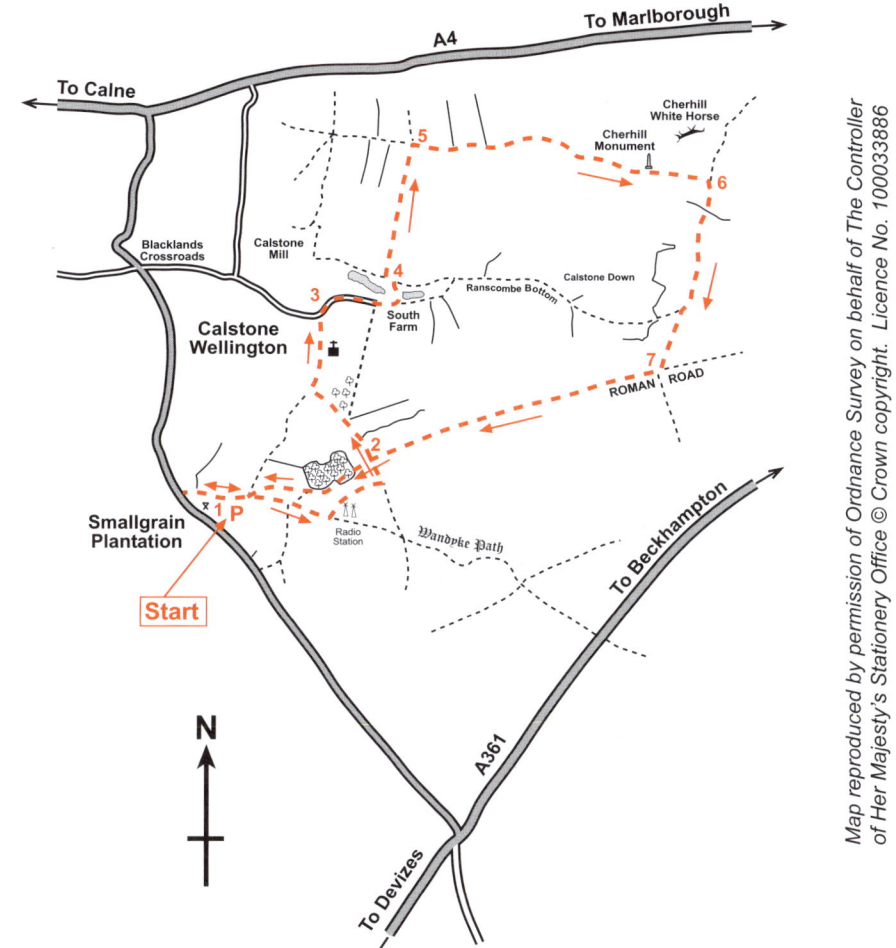

track until Cherhill Monument comes into view. *(Here are good views of the White Horse.)* On L are two gates leading onto the National Trust area. Go through both and keeping fence on R climb to Monument. *(This is 125' high and was built in 1843 to commemorate an ancestor of the Lansdowne family, Sir William Petty. Cherhill White Horse is carved into the northern slope of the hill. This was cut in 1780, is 129 ft long and 142 ft in height and at one time had an eye made of the bottom of glass bottles, which made it sparkle in the sunlight.)*

Follow path that passes directly behind the Monument and goes through gap in side of ditch / bank of hill fort, to meet chalky track coming up from L **(6)**.

Turn R and follow track, which is part of the Wessex Ridgeway, uphill to gate in fence ahead. Go through gate to follow track downhill and through another gate. Continue on this track for about a mile until you reach gate and sign, which reads "Byway" in both directions **(7)**. Turn R onto the Roman Road. This leads back to car park in an almost straight line – about 1½ miles.

Walk 8   Sutton Benger and Christian Malford
contributed by Jenny Cox and Alan Roberts

Starting Point: Sutton Benger Village Hall in Chestnut Road.
Grid Reference: ST 948785
OS Maps: Explorer 156; Landranger 173
Distance: 4 miles or 6 kilometres
Time required: 2 hours
Parking: Hall car park as above.
Bus: Service 91 from Chippenham Bus/Rail stations (not Sundays or public holidays).
Refreshments: The Bell House Hotel and The Wellesley Arms in Sutton Benger.
Introduction: A pleasant walk through a National Trust SSSI (Site of Special Scientific Interest - orchids in Spring) by the River Avon visiting two churches.

Walk Description:

Leave car park **(1)** by gap to L of village hall and into playing field. Follow R hedge to bottom R corner, through gap into next field and continue to hedge ahead and cross bridge. Turn R onto worn path to follow hedge round field to far R corner. Cross bridge but ignore stile immediately on L after bridge. Continue in same direction with hedge on L to stile at far end to enter SSSI. Keep hedge on L and go over stile on L in field corner. Make for distant pylon, passing small pond on L, to gate into green lane leading to Sutton Lane **(2)**.

Take track opposite to cross the River Avon at weir **(3)**. *(From here there are good views of All Saints Church in Christian Malford.)*

Follow green lane and turn L through metal gate, just before brick railway bridge, into field. Follow hedgerow on R to stile into paddock and cross to field gate ahead.

Cross field diagonally towards church to stile/bridge/gate and continue in same direction through horse paddocks with gates/stiles to reach gate into churchyard **(4)**. *(Observe a WWII pill box on L just before churchyard.)*

From church gate at far end of churchyard turn R onto road and after 50 yards cross stile on L into field *(Malford Meadows)*. Cross stile in opposite hedge and make for stile/bridge/stile next to gap in hedgerow. Head for distant buildings.

Go over stile between buildings to L of double telegraph pole to reach main road through kissing gate. Turn L along grass verge to bridge and cross road with care. Over bridge and immediately R over stile **(5)**. Bear L and follow line of telegraph poles to opposite hedge.

Cross stile into next field *(observe another WWII pill box in R corner)*. Make for houses/ track, keeping hedge/poles on R. At bend of track cross stile on R to cross small field and enter car park outside La Flambe restaurant.

Turn L on road, and pass All Saints Church to cross main road. Take small road opposite, passing R of the Bell House Hotel back to village hall.

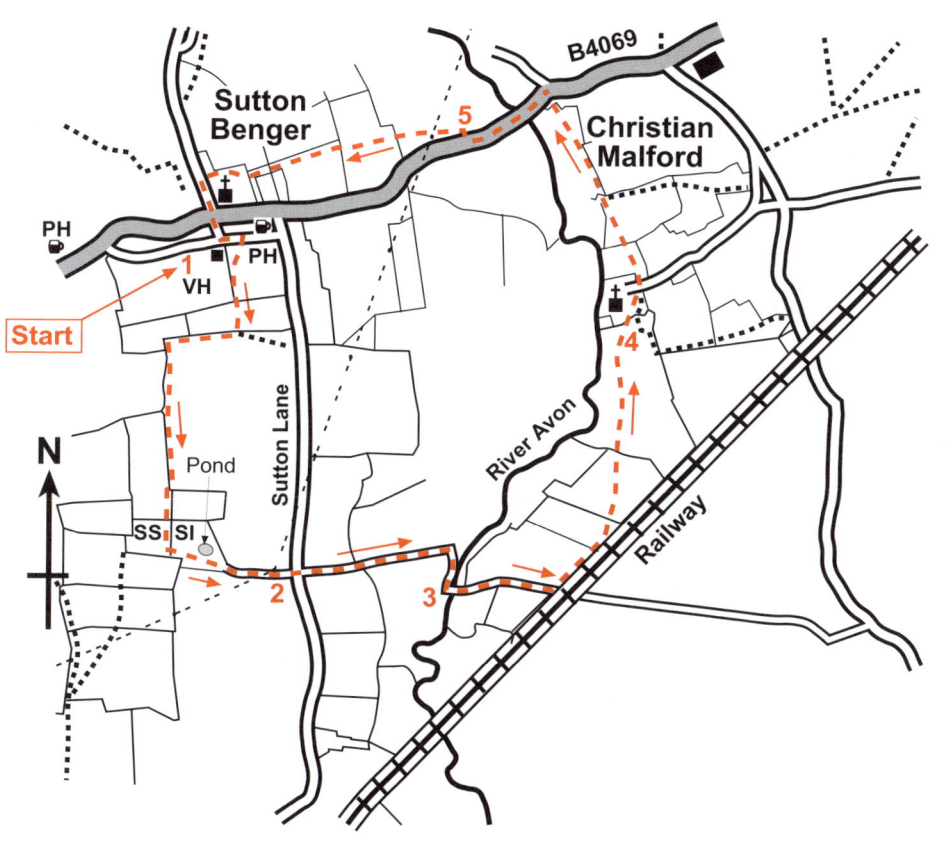

21

Walk 9   Quemerford, Compton Bassett and Cherhill
contributed by David Auld and Alan Roberts

Starting Point:	Large lay-by on south side of A4 before reaching Cherhill from Calne.
Grid Reference:	SU 027698
OS Maps:	Explorer 157; Landranger 173
Distance:	8 miles or 13 kilometres
Time required:	3½ to 4 hours
Parking:	As above.
Bus:	Regular service 42 between Calne and Marlborough. Limited Service X76 between Calne and Marlborough. Alight at Compton Bassett turn or Quemerford Gate.
Refreshments:	Pubs in Compton Bassett and Cherhill.
Introduction:	The early part of the walk, west and north of Cherhill, is on lower and fairly level ground, but after Compton Bassett the land rises to a higher plateau, where long views to the east are possible.

Walk Description:

From eastern end of lay-by **(1)** cross A4 with care and walk between Quemerford Gate farm buildings, keeping converted barn on R. Continue straight ahead through gate to end of track, cross stile on R to reach wooden footbridge, cross and then turn immediately R then L, skirting wooden building to cross stile. Cross track beyond to next stile behind corner of hedge. Cross this stile and follow hedge to R, turning L near corner of field and following that field boundary to cross stile by field gate in corner. Walk along track, go through gap in hedge on R and cross a stile to reach road, and turn L **(2)**.

Continue to road junction, which is the Compton Bassett road, turn R and walk north along this road for 800 yards **(3)**. Turn L onto bridleway and immediately R to follow wire fence on L for approx. 300 yards, then turn L onto gravel cycle track to follow perimeter fence of waste disposal site. Soon after this fence disappears off to L *(Andrews' Patch)*, step over fallen tree trunk and stone piles into field. Turn R onto grassy track along edge of field and follow this as it bends L and goes downhill. Cross stream at bottom and continue ahead on bridleway to R of extensive solar farm. Track soon narrows to become a footpath and ascends. 200 yards beyond brow of hill, turn R through wide gap in hedge **(4)** passing to L of two old oak trees. Continue along hedge beyond, passing gorse bushes and secluded pond on R.

The land starts to drop slightly to meet woodland. Soon after field edge turns L, turn R off it *(effectively straight on)* through small copse and crossing small bridge. Enter field and follow hedge on L to reach track. Turn R and pass house on R, where track becomes a metalled road. *(Note: Path diversion is to L here if sand extraction is approved at Freeth Farm.)* After approximately 150 yards, just before reaching Freeth Farm on R, turn L down bridleway with house on L. Keep on this when it bends L *(north east)*. When track bends sharp R, continue ahead on bridleway through gate and go R diagonally across field to far corner.

Do not take obvious farm gate but go through small wooden gate on its L. Enter small wood to L of gate and take path through it. This skirts the fenced grounds of Manor Farm to R, and there is a stagnant stream to L. *(The path is barely discernible in places and sometimes appears impassable but persevere! It is also riddled with badger setts – **take care!**)*

On reaching metalled road **(5)**, turn R and walk south, passing Austin's Farm to R and Streete Farm dairy to L then several cottages on L. Take clear track to L, adjacent to stone and brick wall, signposted as

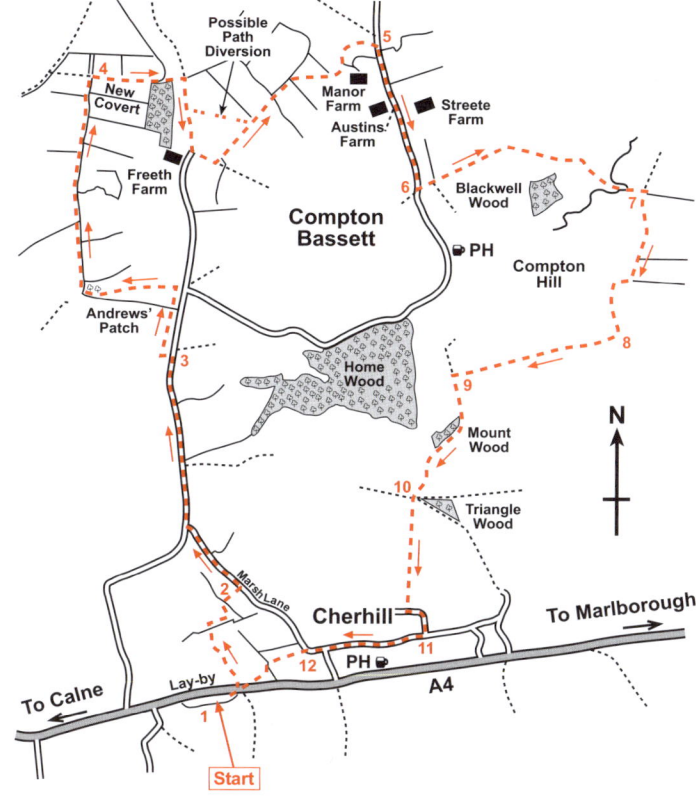

a footpath **(6)**. Follow this track uphill for 400 yards, crossing two stiles. Soon after track goes gently downhill then sweeps L, leave it and head towards a mound 8-10 feet high just ahead and on R. Pass this mound and ascend dry valley beyond. At top, go through small metal gate next to stile to reach T- junction and turn R onto bridleway **(7)**.

Follow this straight ahead, through R then L kinks, to reach crossing of bridleways and turn R **(8)**. From here walk downhill and this bridleway eventually meets another at T-junction **(9)**. Turn L here and walk up green way until reaching fields on L, *(with good views of Cherhill White Horse and Lansdowne Monument)*. Path curls to R here along edge of fields and passes through gates to reach metalled lane, close to house and farm buildings **(10)**. Cross lane to concrete road passing to R of farm buildings. Follow footpath downhill, with fence on R, to gate into double-hedged path which passes children's playground. At bottom turn L into metalled Mill Lane, and at T- junction turn R into Cherhill village **(11)**. Continue along road until reaching last few modern houses at western end of village. Here road veers to R but route is over stile on L **(12)**, where there is a finger post. Go across field towards farm buildings and cross stiles 50 yards to L of gate. Bear L across next field to stile and regain A4. Turn R and follow roadside path until opposite lay-by, cross road with care to starting point.

Walk 10   Lacock, Bowden Hill and Naish Hill

contributed by Jean Drewett and Judy Hible

Starting Point: National Trust car park, Hither Way, Lacock.
Grid Reference: ST 918682
OS Maps: Explorer 156; Landranger 173
Distance: 4 to 5 miles or 6 to 8 kilometres
Time required: 2½ to 3 hours
Parking: As above.
Bus: Regular service X34 from Chippenham Bus Station (not Sundays or public holidays).
Refreshments: Tearooms and public houses in Lacock.
(public toilets in car park behind Red Lion.)
Introduction: An optional circular or figure of eight walk in the picturesque Wiltshire countryside around Lacock. After heavy rain option 1 is recommended.

Walk Description:

Leave car park by entrance gate **(1)**, cross road on zebra crossing and turn R along grass verge. Bear R following curve of road to reach far pavement and turn R. With the Abbey on L proceed along walled pavement towards river bridge. Here there is a railed footbridge before stone bridges crossing the River Avon. **(Care must be taken, as it can be a busy traffic area.)** Continue up hill, passing the Bell Inn on R to reach Bewley Common **(2)** in a further 250 yards.

Take path diagonally across Common, aiming well to L of the gate between pillars indicating an entrance to Bowden Park. After approx. 250 yards, turn L onto stony track leading to walled house with two stone mushrooms in front of it. Take path to R of this house and go through gate/stile. Turn R uphill and follow path round edge of field to arrive at gate/stile at top **(3)**. Cross and continue uphill to next gate/stile. Bear R then L, relentlessly uphill, to go around edge of wood to L. Veer slightly R and away from wood, still uphill, passing to L of small clump of trees. Aim for gap between two woods at brow of hill where there is stile, and from which farm buildings can be seen ahead and to R.

Cross over stile and keep hedge to L walking towards lower end of conifer wood. Follow path through wood to stile on other side. *(Immediately over this, admire panoramic view.)* Ignore gap with remains of gate, and stile, to R and continue ahead with fence to R, going gradually downhill. Some 100 yards past farm on R go over stile on R into lane *(Naish Hill)* **(4)**.

At bottom of hill continue on road straight ahead for 50 yards and go through waymarked gate on L **(5)**. Cross over three fields using stiles or gaps left in electric fences. Aim for five-barred gate with stile next to it to

Lacock Abbey

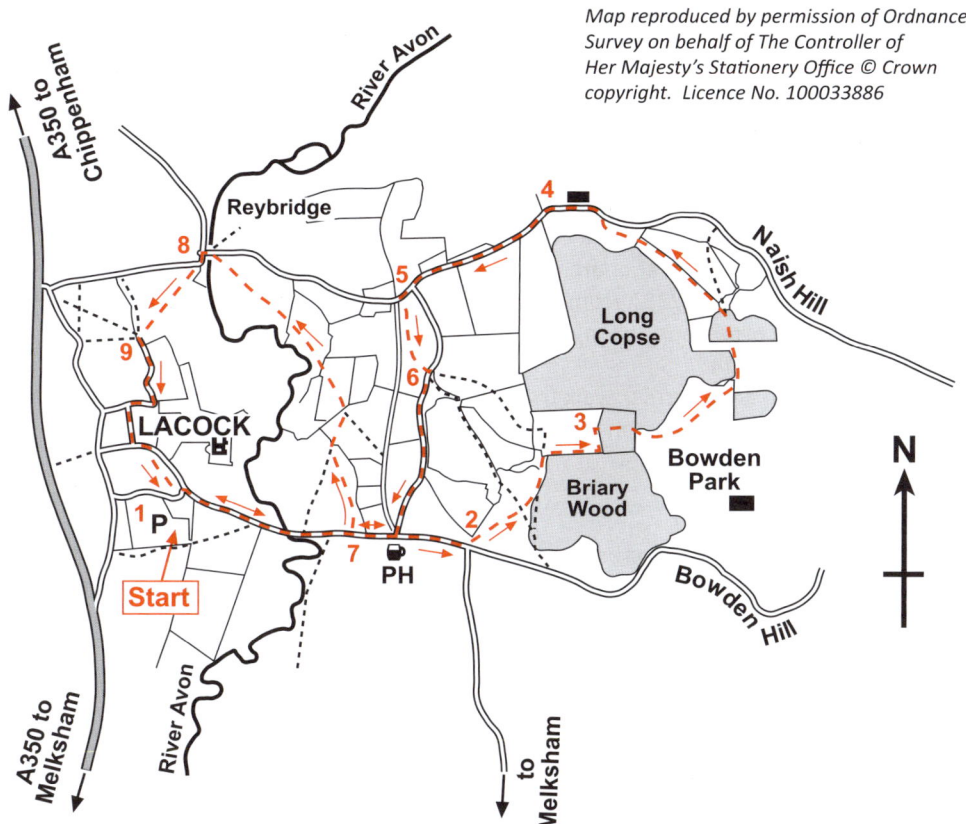

far L of third field, which leads to metalled road **(6)**. Turn R here and pass Bewley Court on R and continue to road junction at Bell Inn.

OPTION 1: Retrace steps downhill to Hither Way car park **(1)** and Lacock village.

OPTION 2: Continue R on road towards village. A few yards past 40 limit sign, there is on R a concealed double stile **(7)**. Go over this and, walking parallel to hedge on R, cross field to wooden footbridge on R. Go over bridge and adjoining stile, turn L along hedge to gap in next hedge. Continue on track between two fields and go down slope at end to cross stile *(this can be very boggy)*. Follow path along bank of the River Avon, crossing stream by means of stile/footbridge/kissing gate en route. When river veers L, go straight ahead across field to arrive at stepless stile into lane.

Turn L to go over bridge across the Avon, and L again at T-junction **(8)**. At bend, turn L between cottages onto tarmac path across field to kissing gate **(9)**. Turn L and walk down to ford, over packhorse bridge and on to the church of St Cyriac. Turn R along street for 50 yards then L at the Carpenter's Arms along East Street, passing village lock-up and tithe barn on L. At end, turn L and walk past the Abbey entrance. Cross road and take path on R through trees to the Hither Way car park **(1)**.

Walk 11   Yatton Keynell and Easton Piercy

contributed by Judy Hible

Starting Point: Church of St Margaret of Antioch, Yatton Keynell (opposite Bell Inn).
Grid Reference: ST 866764
OS Maps: Explorer 156; Landranger 173
Distance: 4 miles or 6 kilometres
Time required: 2 hours
Parking: Roadside near church – please park considerately.
Bus: Service 35/35A from Chippenham Bus/Rail Stations every 2 hours approx. (not on Sundays or public holidays).
Refreshments: Bell Inn.
Introduction: An easy circular walk from the small village of Yatton Keynell out to the hamlet of Easton Piercy – site of a medieval village - over fields and through a couple of woods.

Walk Description:

From the church **(1)** turn L and cross main road to pass Bell Inn, follow pavement on The Street until reaching stone stile on R **(2)**. Walk behind stile on path between houses to kissing gate and bridge. Cross into field, straight ahead across field to stile **(3)**. Straight ahead from stile along LHS of hedge then slightly L to stile in opposite hedge **(4)**. Cross next field very slightly L of straight ahead to another stile **(5)**. Bear L along edge of wood, straight across gravel drive then follow edge of wild boar enclosure and wood on your R.

At the end of wood **(6)** cross stile and bridge to corner of large field, the exit is diagonally opposite corner – either walk directly across or follow RH field margin (depending on state of ground). Cross through gap into next field **(7)**, follow RH field margin to another gap, continue to follow RH field margin and turn L at far end. Look for gap **(8)** on your R before corner of field *(ignore stile straight ahead)*. Once in field, turn L along hedge until you reach gate **(9)**. Pass through gate then head half R to L of house ahead to stile **(10)** onto Grove Lane. *(To your R is the site of the medieval village of Easton.)*

Turn L on lane for 300 yards then bear L through gate **(11)** *(sign on telegraph pole)*. Continue through wood, bear slightly R from hedge line on L and follow signed path to stile into field. Follow RH hedge to gap into next field **(12)**, then bear slightly R to another gap (follow RH hedge if field cropped / ploughed / muddy). Continue along this hedge across another field to stile **(13)**. The route drops down into ditch then straight on across field and through gap in hedge. Continue on this line to facing corner of field and stile to R of gate **(14)**. The stile brings you out on Grove Lane, follow this road as it turns R and comes out onto The Street by the Ebenezer Chapel **(15)**. Turn L and retrace your steps back to The Bell and cross main road to reach the church.

The parish of Yatton Keynell lies in the northern part of Wiltshire, often referred to as the 'Wiltshire Cotswolds' due to its local geology.

The name of the parish was originally Eaton. Henry Caynell had a holding there in 1242 and the inhabitants commonly called it Yatton. Notable Buildings: Church of St Margaret of Antioch – Sir William Keynell built the original church around 1250 for his safe return from a Crusade, rebuilt between 1485 and 1500. The stone chancel screen is decorated with the printed arms of former lords of the Manor: Keynell, Keynes, Gore and Trupendell. It is one of only three in Wiltshire, the others situated at Hilmarton and Compton Bassett. Lion Lodge (formerly Red Lion Inn) C17; The Bell Inn C17; Ebenezer Baptist Chapel 1835.

The hamlet of Easton Piercy is now part of the parish of Kington St. Michael but until late in medieval times was a separate village and parish with its own small chapel, graveyard and cross. The chapel was taken down around 1610. The early name was Easton Piers from the Piers family who owned the manor in the mid-12th century. The present Manor Farm is on the site of Easton Piercy Manor House which was largely demolished in 1630.

Walk 12   Corsham, Easton and Corsham Park

contributed by Bob Howlett and Judy Hible

Starting Point:	Corsham Park car park, Lacock Road, Corsham
Grid Reference:	ST 880703
OS Maps:	Explorer 156; Landranger 173
Distance:	3½ miles or 5.6 kilometres
Time required:	2 hours
Parking:	As above.
Bus:	Regular service X31 between Chippenham Bus/Rail Stations and Bath. Alight in Newlands Road and start walk from St Bartholomew's Church **(22)**.
Refreshments:	Tea rooms and pubs in Corsham. (public toilets in car park by Co-op store)
Introduction:	Mainly parkland and farmland with some lane walking. NB Dogs on leads at all times. Corsham Court has large flocks of sheep, wild geese and swans; adjacent farms have cows, horses and ponies.

Walk Description:

Start from car park on Lacock Road **(1)** - cross road and follow permissive path into Corsham Park. Corsham Lake is ahead - turn R on stony path **(2)**. Over stile, cross drive **(3)** from the Lodge to Lake Cottage and follow fenced footpath to kissing gate **(4)** - straight across field, to stile onto Ladbrook Lane **(5)** - turn L down road past Park Farm and GR post box into Westrop. *(Look out for the yew topiary over the gate to Westrop House on the left.)*

Turn R down drive before no 14 Westrop (FP sign) **(6)**. Pass Rose and Unicorn House and take stile on R **(7)**.

Cross stile and head half L to top left-hand corner of field by oak tree and stone stile **(8)** - straight across field to stone stile **(9)** - cross road following signpost. Then, almost immediately, cross wooden stile **(10)** on L of drive. Cross field to stone stile just to L of no 3 Easton **(11)**. *(Note typical local building style and materials.)*

Cross middle of field, keeping pond hidden by trees on your L, to gap in fence **(12)**.

Cross field half L to stile in top L corner **(13)**. Turn L on Thingley Road and follow verge. *(Look out for ornate gate piers on unused carriage drive to the Park through Mynte Wood.)*

At the A4 crossroads at The Chequers - turn L then L again through kissing gate **(14)** into Corsham Park.

Follow track to kissing gate in metal fence **(15)**. Continue uphill, with row of oaks on your R, to kissing gate **(16)** into Mynte Wood to L. Cross the Dry Arch **(17)** (over carriage drive) to kissing gate **(18)**. Then cross pasture keeping fenced plantation on your L and ditch on your R. *(There is a view across Corsham Lake to Bowden Hill on your left.)*

Continue through kissing gate **(19)** still following ditch, to another kissing gate **(20)**. *(Note the good view of Corsham Court and St Bart's Tower to your right.)*

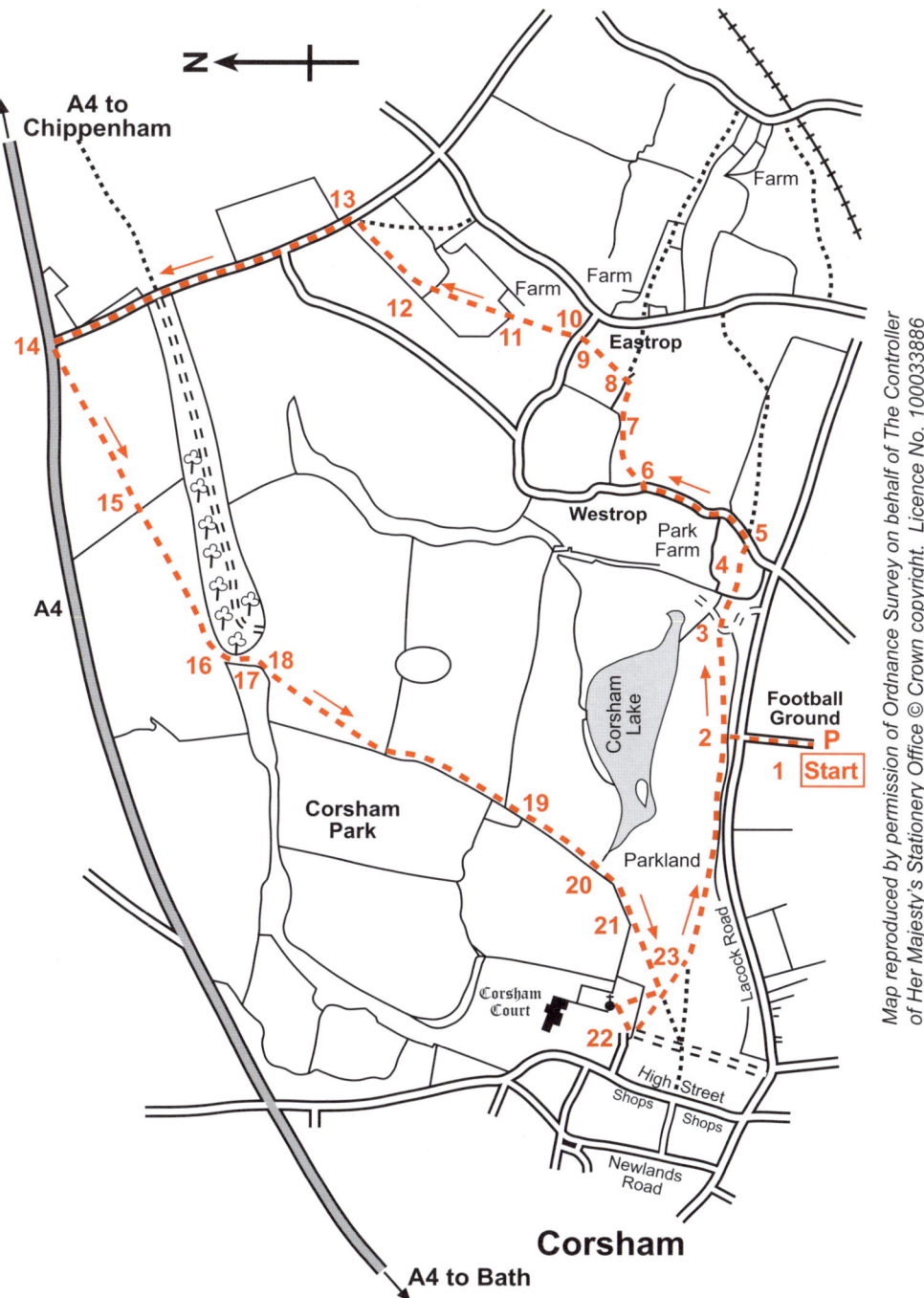

The ditch doglegs **(21)** so path cuts across to corner of the churchyard. Take kissing gate half-way along wall to your R **(22)**. Walk around to back of the church. *(The grave of Sarah Jarvis is behind a yew tree, in line with the church door. Also look for a private entrance from Corsham Court to a door with an 'M' for Methuen above it.)*

A detour through car park and down Church Road will take you to Corsham High Street.

Return to the Park - go straight on until you meet stony path **(23)** then turn L and follow this back to permissive path to car park, with Corsham Lake on your L.

Also available from The North West Wiltshire Group of the Ramblers
12 More Walks around Chippenham

Information on guided walks organised by the Ramblers in Wiltshire can be found at:
www.wiltsswindonramblers.org.uk

YOUR NOTES